Totally WACKY

FACTS ABOUT LAND ANIMALS

CARI MEISTER

CAPSTONE PRESS
a capstone imprint

Vultures PEE ON THEIR LEGS to keep cool.

It's natural AIR-CONDITIONING!

A hot crocodile sleeps with its mouth **WIDE OPEN.**

3

A turkey group is called a **POSSE**, and a peacock group is called a **PARTY**.

A group of kangaroos is called a **MOB**.

A flamingo flock can have up to **1.5 MILLION BIRDS!**

WATCH OUT! A group of rhinos is called a CRASH.

THE CHICKEN IS CLOSELY RELATED TO TYRANNOSAURUS REX.

GREAT UNCLE T.

Why didn't I get those **HUGE TEETH?**

A chicken has a "COMB" on its head and two "WATTLES" under its neck.

Mike the Headless Chicken lived for 18 months without HIS HEAD!

Baby monkeys suck their THUMBS.

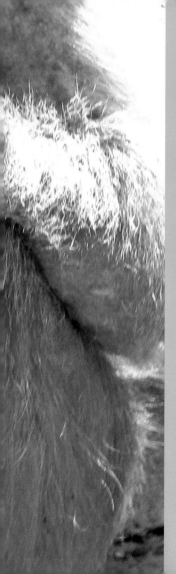

Baby elephants suck their TRUNKS.

Giraffes use their **TONGUES** to clean their **EARS** and **NOSES**.

Orangutans use their **teeth** to clip their **toenails.**

House cats spend 50% of their waking time GROOMING THEMSELVES.

Female REDBACK spiders EAT THEIR MATES.

Darling, will you be my ... LUNCH?

Your what?

Bald eagle partners stay together for a lifetime.

SLOTHS POOP ONLY ONCE A WEEK.

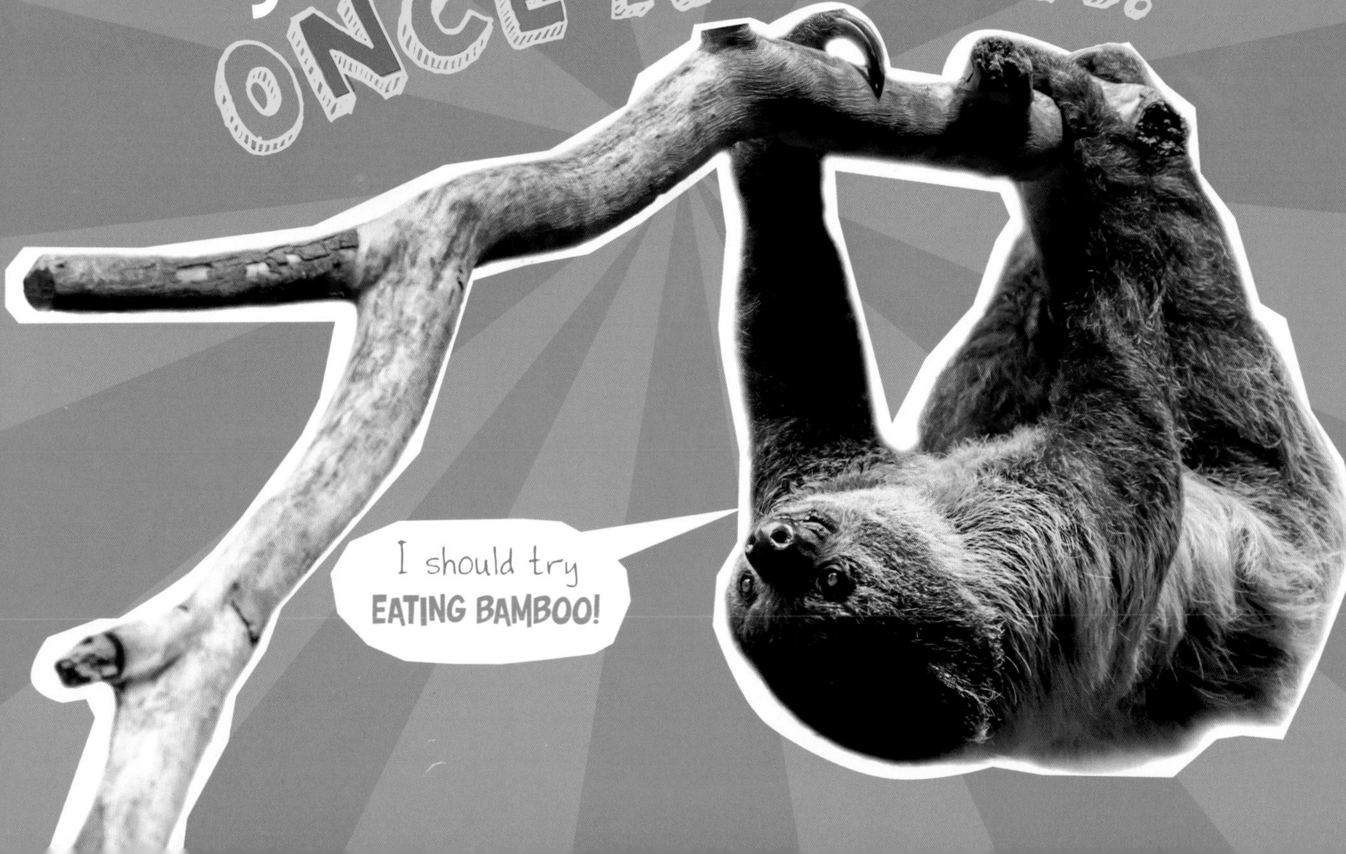

SOME HUMMINGBIRDS WEIGH LESS THAN A PENNY.

A bumblebee bat is the world's smallest mammal. It's as heavy as TWO PAPERCLIPS.

The world's smallest dog, a Chihuahua, can fit in a POCKET.

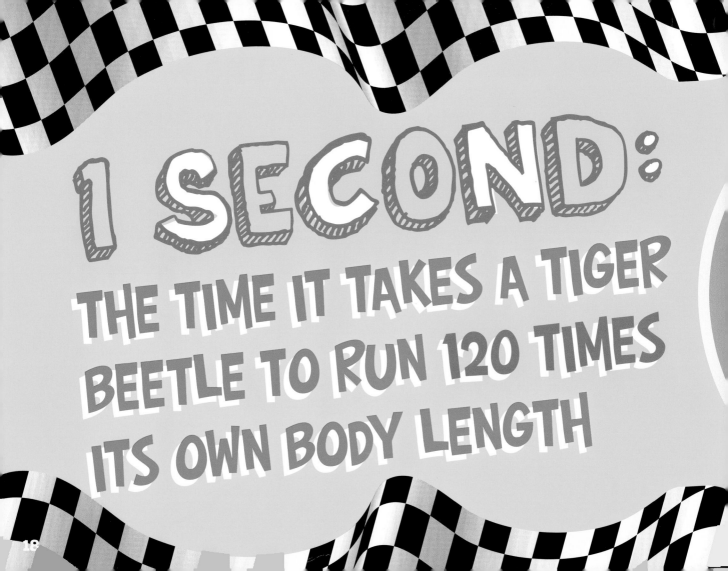

1 SECOND:

THE TIME IT TAKES A TIGER BEETLE TO RUN 120 TIMES ITS OWN BODY LENGTH

The cheetah clocks in as the fastest mammal, running 70 miles (113 kilometers) per hour.

The PEREGRINE FALCON can reach speeds of up to **200 MILES** (322 km) **PER HOUR!**

Pit vipers can see INFRARED.

Rats have an uncanny ability to DETECT LAND MINES.

The greater wax moth can hear sounds at higher frequencies than any other animal.

And you thought I was A PEST?

23

The African drongo bird *mimics* a meerkat's warning call to steal **MEERKAT FOOD.**

24

A hawk moth caterpillar larva looks like **A SNAKE** to fool predators.

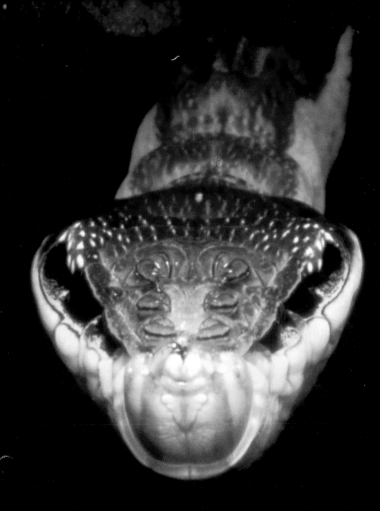

Male "dancing frogs" WAVE THEIR LEGS in the air to ATTRACT FEMALES.

A FEMALE SLUG sometimes bites off a male slug's **PRIVATE PARTS.**

Seriously? AHHHH!

Male porcupines **PEE** on females before **mating.**

HOGNOSE SNAKES

let out stinky **"death"** smells to avoid CAPTURE.

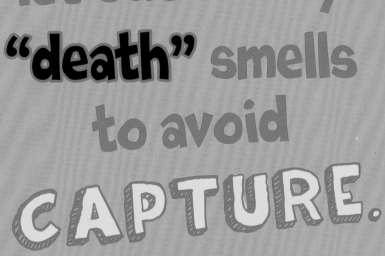

SOME DUCKS PLAY DEAD TO AVOID BECOMING A FOX'S MEAL.

An opossum will PLAY DEAD for hours, even sticking out its tongue for added effect.

Bees and butterflies drink CROCODILE TEARS.

SOME MOTHS HAVE HARPOON-SHAPED MOUTHPARTS TO SUCK TEARS FROM SLEEPING BIRDS.

Some kinds of carpenter ants purposely explode with **TOXIC GOO** to stop predators.

The Moroccan flic-flac spider **BACK-HANDSPRINGS** away from its enemies.

CATCH ME if you can!

HIPPOS FLING POOP AT EACH OTHER WHEN GETTING OUT OF THE WATER.

Flies lay their eggs in rotting flesh.

A JACKAL CUB EATS ITS MAMA'S BARF.

TUSKS ARE REALLY VERY LARGE TEETH.

An elephant's tusks can grow to be 10 feet (3 meters) long.

A cow's udder can hold almost **6 GALLONS** (23 liters) of milk.

Got an **upset stomach?** Try drinking

MOOSE MILK!

Dropping a frog into milk will keep the milk **FRESH.**

An alligator can regrow one tooth 50 TIMES.

A vulture PUKES to keep enemies at bay.

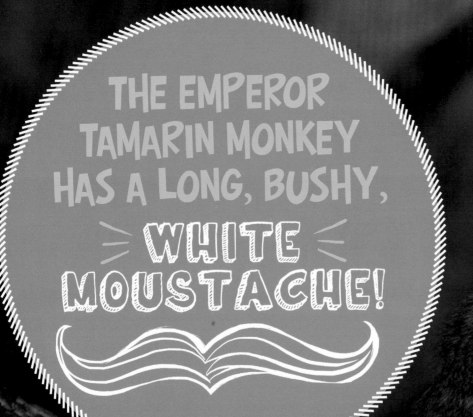

THE EMPEROR TAMARIN MONKEY HAS A LONG, BUSHY, WHITE MOUSTACHE!

A zebra's stripes keep biting flies AWAY.

WANT TO HAVE A SNOWBALL FIGHT? JAPANESE MACAQUE MONKEYS WILL JOIN YOU!

Millions of **monarch butterflies** migrate to the Monarch Butterfly Reserve in Mexico each fall. Trees there **BEND** with the weight of all of the butterflies!

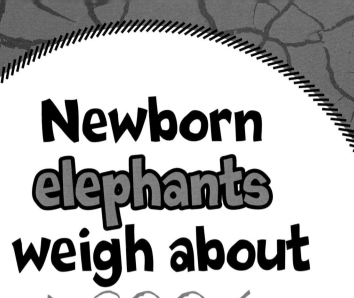

Newborn elephants weigh about 200 POUNDS (91 kilograms)!

A newborn hippo can weigh 110 POUNDS (50 kg).

EGYPTIAN VULTURES USE ROCKS TO BREAK OPEN OSTRICH EGGS.

The American burying beetle buries dead birds and rodents for its BABIES to eat.

Flamingos eat with their heads UPSIDE DOWN.

ELEPHANTS ARE THE ONLY LAND MAMMALS THAT CAN'T JUMP.

A penguin can't fly, but it can JUMP 6 feet (1.8 m) in the air from the water!

The Australian striped rocket frog can jump over 4 FEET (1.2 M).

Kangaroos can't run, but they can travel 25 feet (7.6 m) **IN ONE LEAP.**

THINK FARM ANIMALS ARE BORING?

MUSIC CALMS NERVOUS COWS.

One sheep produces enough wool in a year to make a man's suit.

PIGS CAN'T SWEAT. THEY ROLL IN MUD TO STAY COOL.

61

A dog named **Chaser** has learned to recognize more than 1,000 words.

CROWS MAY BE ABLE TO COUNT.

1, 2, 3 ...

SOME ELEPHANTS CAN BE TRAINED TO PAINT SELF-PORTRAITS.

Rhino horns are made up of the same stuff as your HAIR.

THE NAKED MOLE RAT HAS NO HAIR.

Monkeys pick
(and eat)
BUGS out
of each
other's hair.

POLAR BEAR MAMAS GAIN **400 POUNDS (181 KG)** DURING PREGNANCY.

Mama crocodiles carry their babies around in their MOUTHS.

The yellow ant smells like a LEMON.

One kind of millipede smells like CHERRY COLA.

The hoatzin bird smells like COW DUNG.

A BINTURONG'S BEHIND SMELLS REMARKABLY LIKE BUTTERED **POPCORN!**

MOVIES, ANYONE?

RETICULATED PYTHONS CAN GROW AS LONG AS 32 FEET (9.8 M)!

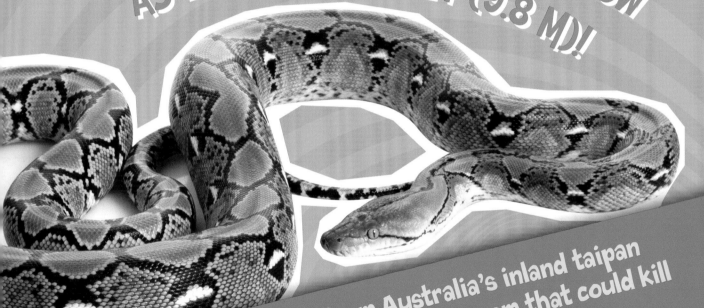

One bite from Australia's inland taipan snake contains venom that could kill 100 adult men.

MANY SNAKES DISLOCATE THEIR JAWS SO THEY CAN SWALLOW LARGE ANIMALS WHOLE.

A CHAMELEON'S EYES CAN LOOK IN TWO DIFFERENT DIRECTIONS.

I've got my eyes ON YOU!

The **horned lizard** can shoot BLOOD out of its **eyes.**

SNAKES DO NOT BLINK.

natural sunscreen droplets

A HIPPO'S SWEAT ACTS AS A SUNSCREEN AND INSECT REPELLENT.

Geckos can REGROW their tails.

If a flatworm is cut in half, each piece will grow into a **new worm**.

TWO DAYS AFTER AN ANT DIES, OTHER ANTS CARRY IT AWAY TO AN ANT GRAVEYARD.

RHINOS COVER THEMSELVES IN MUD TO KEEP BUGS AWAY.

Polar bears have **BLACK SKIN.**

Like its fur, a tiger's skin is **STRIPED.**

A BALD EAGLE'S NEST CAN BE MORE THAN 9 FEET (2.7 M) ACROSS AND 20 FEET (6 M) TALL.

An edible-nest swiftlet makes its nest out of **SPIT.**

SOCIABLE WEAVERS BUILD MASSIVE NESTS THAT HOUSE 400 BIRDS.

Female American sand burrowing mayflies live for less than 5 minutes.

GALAPAGOS TORTOISES CAN LIVE TO BE 150 YEARS OLD.

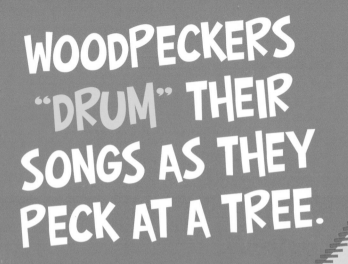

WOODPECKERS "DRUM" THEIR SONGS AS THEY PECK AT A TREE.

HOUSEFLIES HUM IN THE KEY OF F!

Giraffes sleep with their eyes HALF OPEN.

HORSES, ZEBRAS, AND ELEPHANTS SLEEP STANDING UP.

A CAT'S EAR HAS **32 MUSCLES**; A HUMAN'S EAR HAS **TWO**.

90

100,000: the number of muscles in an elephant's trunk

OWLS SWALLOW THEIR FOOD WHOLE AND THEN COUGH UP PELLETS OF BONES AND FUR.

Blister beetles release a chemical used to treat **human warts**.

1,000: THE NUMBER OF MOSQUITOES A BAT CAN EAT IN AN HOUR

Insects have been on Earth for about 400 million years.

A kind of skink lizard has

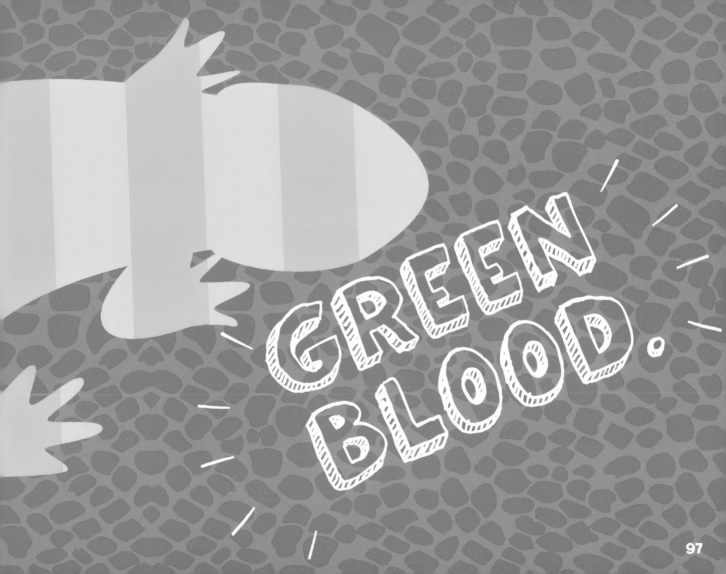

A millipede can have up to 750 legs.

A CATERPILLAR HAS 16 LEGS.

Most spiders have four sets of eyes.

A TARSIER'S EYE IS **BIGGER** THAN ITS BRAIN.

DRAGONFLIES HAVE 360-DEGREE VISION.

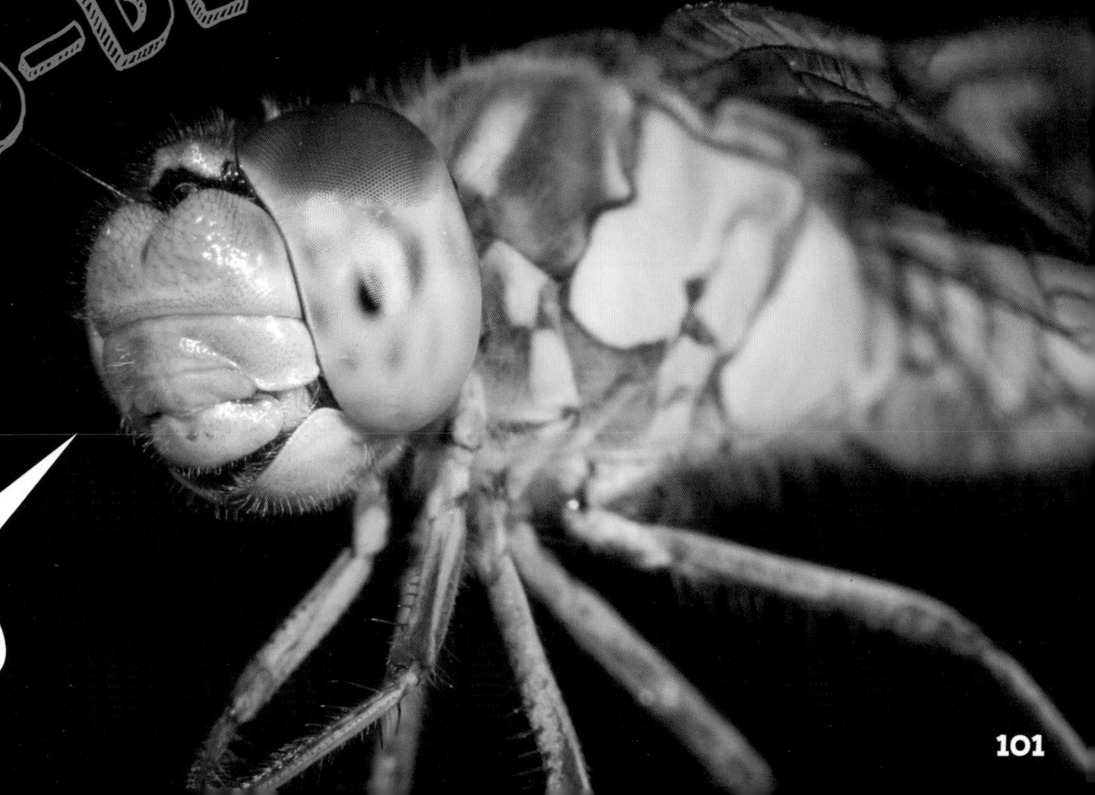

Female mandrill monkeys like males with brightly colored behinds and faces.

MALE FRIGATE BIRDS INFLATE THEIR HUGE, RED NECK POUCH TO ATTRACT FEMALES.

A chipmunk's cheek pouches can hold about 32 beechnuts.

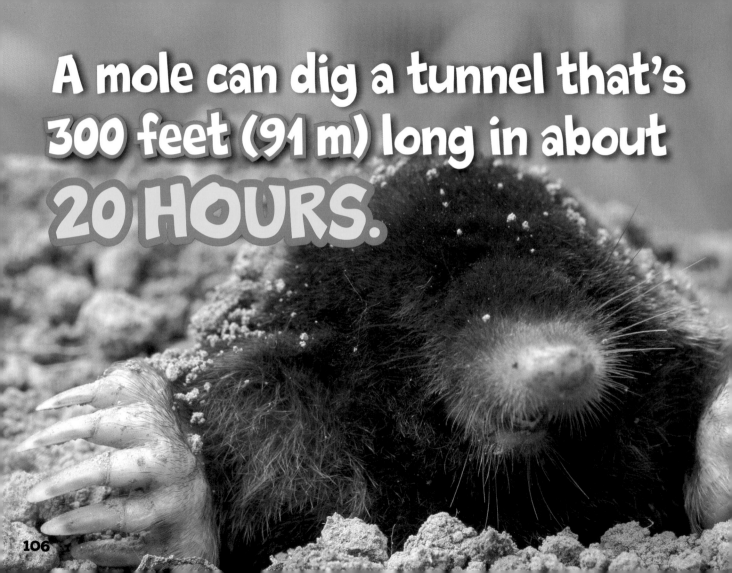

A mole can dig a tunnel that's 300 feet (91 m) long in about 20 HOURS.

ONE UNDERGROUND PRAIRIE DOG TOWN COVERED

25,000

SQUARE MILES (64,750 SQUARE KM)!

THERE ARE **TWO** SPECIES OF ELEPHANTS IN THE WORLD.

FOUR KINDS OF ANTEATERS EXIST.

THERE ARE **EIGHT** TYPES OF BEARS.

400,000 SPECIES OF BEETLES LIVE HERE.

AND MORE THAN 1.5 MILLION KINDS OF INSECTS HAVE BEEN NAMED IN THE WORLD!

GLOSSARY

chemical—relating to the basic substances that make up all materials

frequency—the number of sound waves that pass a location in a certain amount of time

harpoon—a barbed spear used to hunt large fish

infrared—one of the colors of the rainbow that we can't see; infrared is next to red in the rainbow

land mine—an explosive device laid on or just beneath the ground's surface

mammal—a warm-blooded animal that breathes air; mammals have hair or fur; female mammals feed milk to their young

migrate—to move from one place to another

mimic—to copy

pellet—a mass of undigested hair, fur, and bones vomited up by an owl

predator—an animal that hunts other animals for food

repellent—a substance that is able to keep something away

species—a group of animals with similar features

uncanny—beyond what is normal or expected

venom—a poisonous liquid produced by some animals

wattle—extra skin that hangs from the head or neck

READ MORE

5,000 Awesome Facts 2 (About Everything!). Washington, D.C.: National Geographic, 2014.

Peterson, Megan Cooley. *This Book May Bite: A Collection of Wacky Animal Trivia.* North Mankato, Minn.: Capstone Press, 2012.

Ripley's Believe It or Not Kids Fun Facts and Silly Stories the Big One! Orlando, Fla.: Ripley Pub., 2014

INTERNET SITES

FactHound offers a safe, fun way to find Internet sites related to this book. All of the sites on FactHound have been researched by our staff.

Here's all you do:

Visit *www.facthound.com*

Type in this code: 9781491465226

INDEX

Mind Benders are published by Capstone,
1710 Roe Crest Drive, North Mankato, Minnesota 56003
www.capstonepub.com

Editor: Shelly Lyons
Designer: Aruna Rangarajan
Media Researcher: Svetlana Zhurkin
Creative Director: Nathan Gassman
Production Specialist: Lori Barbeau

Library of Congress Cataloging-in-Publication Data
Cataloging-in-publication data is on file with the Library of Congress.
Meister, Cari, author.
Totally wacky facts about land animals / by Cari Meister.
pages cm. — (Mind benders)
Audience: Ages 8-12.
Audience: Grades 4 to 6.
Summary: "Presents more than 100 facts about land animals in a unique layout that appeals to struggling and reluctant readers"— Provided by publisher.
Includes bibliographical references and index.
ISBN 978-1-4914-6522-6 (library binding : alk. paper)
ISBN 978-1-4914-6528-8 (paperback : alk. paper)
ISBN 978-1-4914-6532-5 (eBook PDF)
1. Animals—Miscellanea—Juvenile literature. 2. Children's questions and answers. I. Title.
QL49.M5427 2016
590—dc23   2015016886

Photo Credits
Dreamstime: Daniel Caluian, 43, Joan Egert, 16 (left), P L, 3, Peter Bjerregaard, 89; Getty Images: Claus Meyer, 30—31, Dante Fenolio, 25, David M. Schleser, 29, Merlin D. Tutle, 17 (top), The LIFE Picture Collection/Bob Landry, 7 (right); Minden Pictures: Mark Moffett, 26, Masahiro Iijima, Nature Production, 54, Vincent Grafhorst, 34; Shutterstock: abeadev, 7 (left), Abraham Badenhorst, 44—45, Adam Gryko, 39 (frog), agongallud, 109 (top), Alhovik, 4 (party hat), Alice Mary Herden, 6 (right), Amesan, 91, ANCH, 90, Andy Dean Photography, 5, Apostrophe, 102, Bildagentur Zoonar GmbH, 106, bluedarkat, 4 (bottom), BlueRingMedia, 66 (bottom), bumihills, 63, Caroline Devulder, 109 (back), Cathy Keifer, 72, CyberKat, 21, Dayna More, 100 (right), dedMazay, 78, Dn Br, 24, Dr. Morley Read, 92—93, Edwin Verin, 100 (left), egg design, 27, elnavegante, 16 (right), Eric Isselee, 37, 41, 62, fivespots, 70, Frank Wasserfuehrer, 103, Gualberto Becerra, cover (top right), Hung Chung Chih, 14 (right), Iakov Filimonov, 66 (top), ingret, 11, JGade, cover (top left), Jo Crebbin, 13, John Michael Evan Potter, 83, Jon Beard, 47, koi88, 60, koosen, 17 (bottom), Kuttelvaserova Stuchelova, 86, lendy16, 95 (front), LiliGraphie, 6 (frame), lineartestpilot, 68 (middle), Lisa Yen, 68 (right), lumen-digital, 53, Mackey Creations, 55 (left), makar, 88, mart, 64, Matt Jeppson, 76—77, Matthew Cole, 23 (left), Max Fat, 28, Maxi_m, 108 (right), mayakova, 69 (popcorn), Michael C. Gray, 99, Michael G. McKinne, 2, mountainpix, 74—75, Nagel Photography, 10, nattanan726, 15, Nikola m, 95 (mosquito), NinaM, 40, Noradoa, 50, panbazil (turkey), back cover, 4, panda3800, 4 (top right), PandaWild, 22 (left), pcnorth, 87, Peter Waters, 12, Philip Bird LRPS CPAGB, 80, Photo Africa, 55 (right), photobar, 20—21, photoiconix, 84—85, Radu Bercan, 94, reptiles4all, 22 (right), Robert Eastman, 6 (left), Ron Rowan Photography, 104, Rozhkovs, 42, Sarah2, 19 (top), schankz, 35, Sergio Schnitzler, 8, showcake, 39, Slanapotam, 18, Stephen Lew, 56—57, stockphoto mania, 69 (front), Terry234, 1 (back), 108 (left), Tom Bird, 61 (right), Tony Campbell, 82, tratong, 65, tsnebula23, 71, Vaclav Volrab, cover (bottom right), Vadelma (sunglasses), back cover, 4, Vadim Petrakov, 14 (left), veroxdale, 59, Vital9cbl4, 19 (back), Volkova, cover (bottom left), 23 (right), voylodyon, 101, wawritto, 96—97, Yusak_P, 68 (left); SuperStock: age fotostock, 67, Steve Bloom Images, 49; Wikimedia: Ingo Rechenberg, 33

Design Elements by Capstone and Shutterstock

Printed in Canada.
032015   008825FRF15